The Magnificent You:

A 28- Day Guide to Ultimate Life

By

Tolulope Olaniyan

Terms and Conditions

LEGAL NOTICE

Disclaimer Notice:

Please note the information contained within this document is for educational and entertainment purposes only. All effort has been executed to present accurate, up-to-date, reliable, complete information. No warranties of any kind are declared or implied. Readers acknowledge the author is not engaging in the rendering of legal, financial, medical, or professional advice. The content within this book has been derived from various sources. Please consult a licensed professional before attempting any techniques outlined in this book.

By reading this document, the reader agrees under no circumstances is the author responsible for any losses, direct or indirect, that are incurred as a result of the use of the information contained within this document, including, but not limited to, errors, omissions, or inaccuracies.

Published by Babysteps Publishing Limited

All enquires to kevin@babystepspublishing.com

ISBN- 13-9798771828831

Table of Contents

Introduction

I first came to dwell on the word "the Magnificent me" when I joined the magnificent group created by one of the world's greatest minds, Joseph Mcclendon. He inspired me to write this book to see more value in myself as a black African lady originally from Nigeria residing in Ireland. I was faced with the constant challenge of trying to prove my worth. I realised I didn't have to prove my worth. I should concentrate on being me and appreciate the person I have become, and the light within me will start to shine through. Even though I have been coaching people, have overcome several challenges over the years but it seems my insecurities sometimes come to the surface and tend to dim my light. There was an inner fear of rejection and failure. Of not being able to place the proper value on me. I settled for the available instead of what could be.

It is not that I have not achieved a measure of success, but I just felt things plateaued, and there was no upward motion again. It seems I stopped doing what got me to where I was, and I needed to be reminded of the beautiful piece of creation that I am- a divine masterpiece! This empowered me to kickstart my journey again of living the life of my dream. We are the light of the world; it is our responsibility to allow the light to continue to shine brighter and brighter each day. We are like the city that is set upon the hill and should be visible to all.

The journey to becoming the truly magnificent person you were born to be starts with you. The world will accept any definition we give ourselves. The choice is ours to make. I was out shopping with my daughter one day, and she asked, Mum, why are some clothes so pricy, and others are so cheap? I answered and said to her; it bores down to individual choices. The designers fix their price, and we have no choice but to accept it. Same with us, we can determine what value to place on ourselves.

Negative voices from within and outside will arise, but the most powerful is the one from within you. What are you saying to yourself because this is the major determinant of where you will be? Is your inner voice strong enough to withstand outside pressure?

One of the things I have come to accept is my difference. I have come to accept my strengths and weaknesses. I have identified that excellence is a journey, not a destination, so I continually strive to be a better version of myself. I do not see myself as inferior in any way but am constantly empowered by the realization that I am here for a purpose and fits into the divine agenda of God for humanity. I do not focus on things I do not have but approach each day with a sense of appreciation. Grateful for an opportunity to be simply me. This alone is liberating! I particularly love the song,

"This is me" by "The greatest showman." It is your life; make no apologies for who you are, burst through all the barricades and reach for the sun!

I want to ask you these questions today?

- Are you easily swayed by what people say or think about you?
- Are you allowing people to determine your real worth?

It is time to take the lid off your life. You need to open your eyes to see the possibilities around you. You need to come out of the darkness of the mind that has caged you- start to shine.

My Magnificent Creed

I am truly beautiful- The handwork of a Master Sculpsit

I am born to win- born to reign

I have the power to become who I want to be

I am no ordinary person- I am empowered from a divine source

The source of my strength is rooted in my maker.

I choose today to shine, soar and scale the hurdles

I choose today to live the ultimate life- the life of my dreams because I am truly magnificent.

Why I Wrote the Book

I come from a world where society regard females as less in value than their male counterparts, where it is fine to create double standards, one for a group and one for another. A society where physical and emotional abuse against the female gender is very common. Nigeria, a land full of natural resources and opportunities, yet many people are living in abject poverty. I came to Ireland my new home about nineteen years ago, a beautiful country full of promises and encountered a different kind of prejudice. This coupled with so many other life issues coming at me resulted in emotional trauma about thirteen years ago. I could not cope and therefore slipped into a dark space.

You may never understand the true meaning of freedom until you have experienced imprisonment. We might think being caged is when an individual's freedom is restricted physically. It is even a greater form of imprisonment to be caged by our own minds. Most often, as humans, we think only of the physical body, but we are the sum of the mind, spirit, and body. The mind is the connection between the physical and spiritual whatever impacts on the mind affects the spiritual and the physical.

Flashback

Why does everything seem dark and distant? Like the world is standing apart and aloof. I felt a sense of trepidation and emptiness. Perhaps if there is a little sunshine, a ray of light, just a tiny bit, I might have the courage to continue. I do not understand. Could it be my mind playing a trick on me? What if this was another world, removed from everyone else? Could I be dead and not realize it? Help, somebody wake me up from this nightmare!

Those were my thoughts thirteen years ago in my dark space. I started to query, why me? My life became like a movie; I was the dominant figure, but I could not even recognize myself because that person had no resemblance to the real me. That person was dull, anxious, depressed and lost. She struggled to come out of the darkness around her as her mind became a weapon of punishment, inflicting unending pain, causing countless sleepless nights.

The Turning Point

Hope came from a doctor who said, "you are in perfect health" My mind initially could not accept that at first because it was used to negative. I tried to argue, and he said, I could place you on antidepressants if you wish but do you want to use it for the rest of your life? Whatever you are feeling is not life-threatening; if you don't feed it, it will go.

The experience led me to another journey of self-discovery, emotional mastery, personal transformation, and life coaching. In my years of coaching, I have seen people struggle with many issues that are preventing them from living the ultimate life. I have therefore put this book together to help as a twenty-eight-day guide to dealing with these common issues and give you the tools you need to become the truly magnificent person you are born to be.

Today I challenge you, do not accept the negative stereotypes placed upon you by virtue of your background, society, religion, race, or educational background etc. All may not be working according to plan now but don't be discouraged. The greatest misfortune is if you give up on yourself. Because if you do, who will believe in you? If you quit in the middle, get back in line and if you drop out of the race, start again!

There are also people who have lost hope completely, and it is so difficult for these people to see the possibilities around them. Such need to come out of the recess of their mind, to break the chain of impossibilities and barriers. You can't remain in the dark anymore; the world is waiting for you to manifest your true potentials.

Arise and become the magnificent person you are born to be!

Who Is the Book For?

The book is for people looking for inspiration on how to move their life forward and live the life of their dreams. It is divided into 28 chapters to help with a month of daily inspiration. Creating the change, you need in 28 days.

Many people don't have time to read through books and materials because of the avalanche of information out there. This book is designed with such people in mind- straight to the point with quick reflection exercises each day to help you get results.

Getting results is a matter of what you do with the information in the book. People often look for complex data and think that common sense and fundamental life principles don't work anymore. The truth is that people are using these simple but life-changing principles to transform their lives, and I hope you are one of these people.

While I understand there are different people at different positions in their life journey, but the truth is we all need to be constantly motivated. Iron sharpening each other to keep the edges sharp. So, it does not really matter at what stage you are. You can still benefit immensely from this book.

How to get value from the book

Commit one month – a day each to reading and reflecting daily on what you have learned.

Jot down particular words, phrases or sentences that resonate more with you and see why it stands out from others.

Please do not rush the book but think it through, work on the daily reflections, and add your notes.

Go back to areas where you think you require help and note these to find solutions because they may be what is hindering your growth.

Finally, if you are one of those who seem to have all the answers and cannot learn anything from anyone else, the book is not for you.

Day 1

The Question of Identity

The journey to living our ultimate life and becoming the magnificent person we were born to be starts with an important question: Who am I? Why am I here? And where am I going?

Who am I is the question of Identity?

Our identity differentiates us from others. It comprises of our memories, experience, feelings, thoughts, relationships, and values. Understanding who you are is essential as this determines your daily decisions about yourself, how you take actions and the type of actions you take. Your identity is your brand. It is the most influential factor in your psychology, and most times, we are conditioned by who we think we are.

Most of us over the years have learnt to take the cautious route in carving an identity for ourselves because of past failures, negative experiences, and stereotypes, and this has made us think of ourselves less than we should think.

To move past where you are now, you must see yourself the way God has created you but not as people see you. Everything he has created is beautiful. You need to internalise this and let it register in your subconscious until your conscious mind does not query it anymore. I remember that during the time I experienced trauma, I would wake up with every symptom in the book. I would stand in front of the mirror and call my name "Tolu, there is nothing wrong with you, and you are in perfect health" I kept saying this to myself until it became registered in my subconscious.

Tony Robbins once said, *"the strongest force in the human personality is the need to stay consistent with how we see ourselves"* This is so true because everything we do after that goes to prove how we have identified ourselves. It thus means that how you look at yourself will ultimately reinforce the action you take to maintain that image you have about yourself.

Can I change my identity?

While you may not change who you are as a person, you can modify your identity by changing your behaviour and habits. This is what growth is about, refusing to stay small. Make sure you are constantly developing yourself by pushing yourself and maximising your potentials. Doing things, you have not attempted before, taking on challenges, and moving past your fears. It is often said that many people have not utilised 10% of their potentials, and extraordinarily successful people have allowed themselves to grow by constantly pushing themselves and thus expanding their identity.

No matter what you say to people, if you are not solving their problems or getting results for them, they will not change their perspective about your identity. It would help if you got to a position where you not only consistently deliver but over-deliver.

Reflection

Take time to think about who you are and establish if you are truly living your ultimate life.

Exercises

Write three things down about yourself you believe to be true

Write three things about yourself you don't believe to be true

Day 2

The Question of Why I Am Here

E veryone on this earth has been created for a purpose. Just as our personality differs, so is the problem we are called to solve. Our purpose is a determinant of who we are. It empowers us; it gives us a reason to live.

Living your ultimate life requires you to live your life on purpose. Highly successful people are people who have identified their purpose in life and have acted. You are called to solve a problem and reach out to a particular group; if you fail to identify your purpose, you will never solve the problem you are created to solve. Your purpose is different from your talent. Your talents are identified by your natural abilities, gifts, what you do so well, and what people can identify you with. However, your purpose represents your why?

15

It is important that you find your purpose and live it because other lives are tied to your success. I always visualise the world as a giant puzzle where everyone is part of that puzzle representing different shapes, sizes, and colours. If you take out just one piece, the picture is incomplete, and that is why you matter. No matter what you are told or what you have been made to believe. Your contribution is important because no one can ever replace you. Nobody talks exactly like you, sing like you, look like you, do things exactly as you do, and nobody has a right to think less of you because you can only compare yourself with yourself.

Some have identified their purpose, and to some, this is still difficult. The good news is it does not matter. It is better late than never. Don't say I have always been in this job, business, academics, training, ministry, and it is too late to retrace my step. Never say never, as it is never too late to turn back in the right direction. Imagine going on a journey, and you missed your way. The fact that you have been travelling in the wrong direction for a long time does not mean you are getting closer to your destination. Change your route!

How to find your purpose

I was delivering a talk to a group of young people on "finding your purpose", and someone asked, does your purpose find you or do you find your purpose? My answer is, it could happen either way. In my case, my purpose found me when I was down there in my period of trial and affliction; I knew one thing, I don't ever want anyone to go through what I went through. I discovered coaching in the process and knew that was where I belonged. I am a qualified financial adviser and business specialist. Still, I continue to support people through words of encouragement and coaching, and it has become a way of life for me.

People are going through life working at jobs they hate; stuck in relationships they are unhappy with and living each day as it comes without hope for the future; it is time for you to ask that vital question- what is the meaning of life? Often the answer is within you; when you connect to your maker through the spiritual, he will guide you to your purpose. When you learn to depend on the source and the giver of life, he will lead you on the right path.

Your creator has not left you clueless as to why he has created you- your talents and gifts are also indicators of what he wants you to do. Just as there is nothing that has been created that is useless, so are the gifts that have been deposited in you are there to serve a purpose. It is thus our duty to harness these gifts to solve the problems in the world and leave it better than we met it.

Refection

Think deeply about your life at this stage. Are you genuinely happy doing what you are doing?

Is there something you would love to do but have not started?

Exercise

Try and answer these questions as best as you can.

- What things do you like to do naturally? List the three most important
- What can you give your full concentration to? List the three most important
- What do people easily notice about you? List the three most important

- What drives your passion or keeps you motivated?
- What positive things do you dwell on constantly?
- What arouses your emotions?
- What kinds of thoughts are you most comfortable with?
- What drives your enthusiasm?
- What kind of people would you want to associate with in future?
- Who is your role model?
- If you had all the resources in the world, what would you do with it?
- What makes you happy?
- What do you love to read about?

Day 3

Where Am I Going

Where there is no vision, the people perish." - Proverbs 29:18

This is so true! Imagine you are going somewhere, but you don't know where? And what if you know where you are going but don't know how to get there?

To become truly magnificent and live the ultimate life, we must carefully consider where we are going and establish the path to follow.

There are different routes to a destination in life's journey, and you need to establish the best for you.

Two years ago, I bought this new car to celebrate my birthday and was so delighted with all the extra features on it but refused to familiarize myself with it. I set out on a journey outside my county and decided to use the navigator on the car- I could not figure it out, and I was already getting late, so I decided to go back to my old and reliable google maps on my phone. I was so happy to see my car indicating directions to follow and just did not check to see my phone again. To my surprise, it kept adding time to my journey until I realized they were synchronized alright but working in the opposite direction. Please don't ask me why because I don't have the answer either.

Did I arrive late at my destination? You bet I did; an hour was added to a 10-minute journey! A lot of people move around in circles because they did not establish their route.

I have seen talented and gifted people who are not living the life they are supposed to live because of a lack of clarity of what they want. These people are easily influenced by popular professions, and you can see them move from one career or course to the other. They are in different unrelated businesses at the same, jumping from one boat to the other. They forget that proficiency and reward come from the concentration of effort on one thing at a time.

So how does someone develop a clear vision about what they want?

The first thing you want to do is spend quality time with yourself to reflect. Then write down your vision and state it clearly on a journal or vision board. Visualize the kind of life you want in the form of a picture or diagram. One way to do this is to look at your life in the next five years and imagine how you want it to look. Write or sketch it, your career, education, relationship, family, business, health. Every area of your life should be included. You can use the vision board for clarity. Make collages of the kind of life you want and hang them strategically to remind you of what is important to you. It will help guide your future decisions. *"Write the vision; make it plain on tablets, so he may run who reads it. - Habakuk 2: 2b*

I have heard people say so many times, "I really don't know what I want and where I want to go," and they seem to be really disturbed by it. I understand the frustration; I have been in the same boat before. However, don't put yourself under any pressure. It will all come to you with time. Just make sure when you are inspired, you write it down. It takes time to connect all the dots because it is the most important decision of your life. You want to get things right. You are thinking, what if I make a mistake? What if I choose the wrong vision? What if pursuing that vision is a waste of time? Or what if you reach it and are disappointed because it's not what you expected it to be? We must, however, aim high irrespective of how we feel. *"The greatest danger for most of us is not that our aim is too high, and we miss it, but that it is too low, and we reach it."* – Michelangelo

In order to create the ultimate life, you should not limit your choices to what you think is achievable; try and stretch yourself beyond; Knowing you have great potentials that are yet untapped. *"If you limit your choices only to what seems possible or reasonable, you disconnect yourself from what you truly want, and all that is left is a compromise".* - Robert Frizt

There are times you feel you must sacrifice your dreams to accommodate your family, which is acceptable but don't bury your dreams because you would never be truly happy.

"Cherish your visions and your dreams as they are the children of your soul, the blueprints of your ultimate achievements." - Napoleon Hill

Reflection

One way to think about our vision is to fast forward to the future to the death bed. Ask yourself the question, what things would you regret not doing if you are about to be called home to your maker?

Also, think about how you would like to be remembered.

Exercise

What if money was not a problem and you had all the resources you needed? What do you see yourself doing?

Day 4

How to Get to Your Destination (Goals)

To create your ultimate life and become magnificent, you must have a plan. It is like planning the route to your journey. You are sure of why you are making the journey (Purpose). You know exactly where you are going (Vision). You need to know how to get there (Goal)

Goal setting is so important in life coaching to evaluate results. You want to achieve your ultimate weight; you set goals. You want a promotion at work or change career or job; you set goals. It is like having a life plan. This part of your journey is so crucial as it is where you strategise on how and when?

In setting goals, it is important to set SMART goals. It should also not be too easy; otherwise, you will not be stretching yourself. It is also crucial to make

27

sure that your goals are something that you really would like to pursue and not something that sounds nice aloud or on paper. *"It's better to be at the bottom of the ladder you want to climb than at the top of the one you don't." ~ Stephen Kellogg*

Once you have verified what the goal is and that it is feasible, you need to compare it to your ethical and moral standards. Is it something that you would be proud of? Your values are fundamental, and they provide your drive and motivation. Your goals must be consistent with who you are and what you want to become. If you are setting your life goal, you will also have to set milestones in your goal to make sure that you are making progress.

A common goal-setting technique involves the acronym SMART—

☐ **S**pecific
☐ **M**easurable
☐ **A**ttainable
☐ **R**ealistic
☐ **T**imely

First, you want your goal to be specific. A specific goal sets you up for success and gives you the ability to accomplish it. It also means you'll recognise it when you achieve the goal. Think like a reporter when you're setting a specific goal, asking yourself who, what, where, when, why and, instead of how, which. (Meaning which requirements and constraints can you identify?)

Second, it should be measurable. What numbers can you assign to your goal to measure your progress and attainment? This will help you stay on track and give you a reason to celebrate when you accomplish the goal.

Next is to verify your goal is attainable - identify the steps you'll take to achieve your goal and the time frame involved.

Then comes "realistic," as you want your goal to represent an objective that's not only attainable but also, you're willing to work towards it. At the same time, don't make it easy but something that will represent progress and growth on some levels, say personally and professionally.

Finally, it should be timely. You must give a specific time of completion; otherwise, you do not create a sense of urgency for the execution of your goal. It is paramount for you to anchor your goal within a specific timeframe. To give it a chance of successful execution, you can ask yourself these questions. What must happen to accomplish my goals considering both things within and outside your control.

Just a note--the T in SMART can also stand for tangible. A goal is tangible when you can experience it with one of your five senses. Some say that you have a better chance of making it happen if you think tangible because it will become more "real

"All who have accomplished great things have had a great aim, have fixed their gaze on a goal which was high, one which sometimes seemed impossible."
—Orison Swett Marden

Reflection

Have you considered how you want to accomplish your vision and when? What picture of the magnificent you do you have in mind? Like your vision, you need to write down your goals. Your goal is like your navigator, and you can quickly identify when you are lost. Your goals solidify the fulfilment of your purpose by bringing your efforts in a direction that is consistent with your purpose. When you have goals, it clearly identifies what your focus should be.

Exercise

I am assuming at this stage; you have a picture of where you are going on either a journal, vision board or tablet. Now write down your goals and make sure they are *Specific, measurable, achievable, realistic and time bound.*

Day 5

What is Your Decision - Success is a Choice?

You are created to succeed irrespective of what you are told. There is a higher being, the source of infinite power, who made us in his image and likeness. He gave everyone the opportunity to become truly magnificent and shine. However, he will not force anything on us; thus, he gave us a free will of choice. He does not make decisions for us- we make our decisions. We are universally guided by principles and reap the reward of our actions.

We are created for love but, over time, embrace fear. Fear precedes failure. Fear listens to what people say and internalises it. You can take ordinary things people don't value and turn them into something valuable. It is entirely our choice!

In the words of David Brinkley, "A successful man is one who laid a firm foundation with the bricks others have thrown away". It is about doing the impossible, taking things people consider of no value and making something extraordinary out of it. -The stone which the builder rejected becoming the chief cornerstone.

Some say we have no control at all over our life situation, and fate determines all. I believe there are some things we have no control over, but there are so many things within our control and likewise so many resources to help us achieve the success we truly deserve. As I said, it is truly up to us what we choose to do.

How we interpret and respond to circumstances and events around us is crucial. If we see things always in a negative light, then we would never be able to see the other side of things. There are two sides to a coin; it depends on the side of the coin facing up. I believe all experience is to teach a valuable lesson. Sometimes we win, and other times we learn. The important thing is using circumstances as building blocks for success and not repeating the same mistakes. An easy life was never promised, only that we will develop the strength to pass through it and hopefully learn the lessons from the experience and build our character.

Reflection

What you think about your next step is important. Ask yourself why do you want to succeed? This is so important as a lot of people do not have an emotional connection to what they want to achieve.

Exercise

List 3 things that would happen if you do not realise your dream

Write down the names of people that will be directly impacted

Day 6

The Mind as a Source of Divine Power

L ike I had previously mentioned, our mind is the connection between the body and the soul - It is extremely powerful. As the engine that drives the body, it is the focal point of our life. It, therefore, needs to be guarded like a garden, nurtured, fenced, and protected. If you allow garbage into your life, the result will be garbage life. All issues pertaining to life originate from the mind. Our mind can bring us success or failure, joy or pain, peace, or fear. It can also become a weapon of oppression or freedom. Our minds can liberate or imprison. It all depends on what thoughts you allow. The principle of cause and effect governs our mind, "Whatever a man sows, that he shall reap"

A noble person is a product of beautiful thoughts; an Iconic life is the product of positive, creative ideas. To become magnificent, you must think you are. Our mind is also wired to produce pure loving thoughts. When we think negative, there is an imbalance in the body, and the effect is negative circumstances and diseases. When you are happy, you are full of energy, and the opposite is when you are unhappy, your mood is low so is your energy. Depression and anxiety are diseases of the mind that creeps in from negative thoughts which were allowed to flourish. In cognitive behavioural therapy, a patient is asked to replace old limiting thoughts with a positive one to give the mind a chance to establish a healthier thinking pattern.

Even though our mind is the engine that runs the body, we are the driver of the machine. It means we are not helpless observers but the controller of the mind. We have the power to turn our life around only if we know how to do it. By consistently applying the right thoughts to our life and circumstances, it is possible to change things in your favour, turn situations around and live the ultimate life you desire. Suppose you are experiencing any discomfort or pain in any area of your life. In that case, there is a lack of harmony or balance in that area, and you can change that situation by changing the way you view that situation and start applying positive thoughts. To become the magnificent person you are created to be, you must not allow negativity into your life.

Our minds must feed on positive, edifying, uplifting and joyful things. That is the fuel the engine called the mind need to work efficiently. It must not be polluted with fear, envy, jealousy, and bitterness. It is like using polluted fuel; it will eventually knock the engine. If you, therefore, don't like your life, change your thoughts. A defective engine machine cannot run effectively and efficiently.

One of the things I learnt to change in my life that helped me tremendously is the interpretation I give to things. Things are not often the way they seem, and over time, based on experience, we have developed a lens through which we look at life. A lot of times, things are neither bad nor good. It is the interpretation or meaning we give to it. Often, we need to step out of our past hurts and pains to see the world as it is truly. You will find out you may be wrong about a lot of things based on assumptions you made.

Reflection

Our mind is indeed very powerful, the centre of transformation. It needs the right nourishment to flourish.

Exercises

Think about what thoughts constantly occupy your mind and dwell on them for a few minutes.

Write down the thoughts and keep a journal of these thoughts over a week to see if there is a pattern and triggers.

Day 7

You Are What You Think You Are

Renewing the mind is an important part of creating the life we desire. If we are not happy with our life now, we must change our thoughts. Our life is a true reflection of our inner thoughts and habits. This is brought about in two ways: firstly, all our actions are unconsciously influenced by our inner thoughts, which ultimately attract an environment like our thoughts. Secondly, we send out silent and invisible vibrations which affect others. These vibrations can either attract or repel people. Likes attract likes! You are drawn to people who are like you, and that is why they say, show me your friends, and I will tell you who you are.

Ultimately, if our thoughts and mental attitude are of the wrong type, we will not attract the right kind of people into our lives, and the same is true the other way around. The soul tends to attract what it is focused on. It may be what you fear, love, or cherish. It only needs to be your dominant thought for you to attract it. Every thought is like a seed in the garden called the mind. If you allow it to germinate, it will bring seeds of its own kind, either good or bad. Good thoughts will produce good fruits, and bad or negative thoughts will produce bad fruit. To truly shine and become magnificent starts with the right mindset.

Often, we want to blame our environment, circumstance but we are the architect of our future, the builder of our destiny. We are not as powerless as we think. What we sometimes call failure is oftentimes a manifestation of our weaknesses. Our inability to master our life and emotions. It is common to say organisations hire attitude. No matter how brilliant you are, without the right attitude, you will not get far. People suffer from their lack of commitment, bad decisions, poor service, wrong disposition and most often play the victim game.

They blame everyone but themselves for the results they are getting. It is difficult to help a man who is not ready to help himself. I have had people come to me to be mentored, and one of my processes of sifting people out is by asking them to buy my book on Amazon; the kindle edition cost about £3. Many did not come back again! It is fine for me to invest my time in them, but they are not willing to invest £3 to buy a book that will teach them the knowledge acquired over the years.

It is so true to say as a man thinketh in his heart, so is he. To really become the truly magnificent person you are born to be. You must totally purge your mind of any form of negativity. You need to renew your mind with words that will strengthen you spiritually and emotionally.

You can renew your mind through connecting with the divine source and creator, learning his ways, understanding his instructions, and walking under his divine guidance. Modern technology and advances in neuroscience also proved that it is possible to change or renew the mind. To change a way of thinking, you must create a new path of thoughts because the mind always wants to go into its default thinking pattern. It is just an easy thing to do. It is like taking already established footpaths instead of selecting new ones.

The same way the old path was made, a new one can be made by consistently and deliberately replacing old negative thoughts with new positive ones until they are firmly planted.

Neuroplasticity is the brain's ability to restructure itself through practice and continuous training, leading to new pathways being created in the human brain. Neuroplasticity is what makes personal growth and development possible. This is a proven fact; it is not a myth or theory. It was initially believed that the brain developed in the formative childhood years and then hardened. However, science has proved otherwise. In fact, science has shown that changes can occur in the human brain in little as seven days.

Changing is not just changing the things outside of us. First of all, we need the right view that transcends all notions, including of being and non-being, creator and creature, mind and spirit. That kind of insight is crucial for transformation and healing.-Thich Nhat Hanh

Reflection

If you must change your life, you must change your thoughts. You can only change your thoughts when your mind is renewed. It is a regenerative process that is proven scientifically. Your life now is the sum- total of the quality of your thoughts. It is like looking in the mirror at your own reflection. The reflection of your mind is your life!

Exercises

Take a mirror and look at yourself- what do you see? Remember, your life reflects your thoughts.

Day 8

Go The Extra Mile

The journey may be hard; it is never easy to stand out; you need to go further than everybody else, focus more than everybody else, take the risk others are not willing to take, make the move others are not willing to make, take the chance others are not willing to take.

Sometimes you are totally scared- it is alright. Sometimes you can't go anymore, so you need to surround yourself with people who can motivate you and not discourage you. Don't be afraid to ask for help to remain strong. Sometimes you just need to hear the word to make you go on.

You need a thirst – a hunger for the fulfilment of that dream to become that magnificent person you were born to be. You need to say positive things to yourself to help you take on the challenges that life throws out at you. Just when you feel you have everything figured, then life throws at you a curveball, and it is like you want to crawl again into a corner.

The truth is you are not alone. A lot of people have been in that same situation. You can draw your strength from their stories that you can also come out of the rot and become the magnificent person you were born to be. If there is a will, there is a way. One thing you should never do is to get discouraged that you stop acting. When Life throws dirt at you, dust yourself and get up again- Raise your shoulders up and proceed again on your journey.

Getting up again is so crucial for one is so important for one who wants to make his life worthy of respect and live the ultimate life will be confronted with difficulties. Life is designed to weed out the weaklings and people who do not have enough faith and courage to fight back. The period also helps to build character and strength. This can be likened to the gold refining process; passing through fire helps in refining you to become the magnificent person you are born to be and live that life of your dreams.

Someone once asked me, why can't life be easy? Why do we have so many obstacles? The answer is life is about the survival of the fittest and awards the spoils to those who exhibit faith, courage, steadfastness, patience, perseverance, persistence, cheerfulness, and strength of character, generally.

Reflection

Most times, we think we cannot deal with certain things in our lives, but we can. We have probably overcome so many challenges in our lives before. To live our ultimate life, it is important we don't allow our current situation to overwhelm us.

Exercise:

Make a note of all the challenges you have overcome before and how you did.

Review whatever situation you are going through now and how you can apply the lessons from the past.

Day 9

You Get Back What You Give

Is this true? YES, it is! I can tell you this based on my life experience. When I lived in a time characterised by lack, I noticed one thing. I hoarded more than what was necessary. When I say this, the natural tendency is to think of money and material things alone. What about our gifts and talent? Those things God has given to provide solutions to the challenges of humanity, if you are not making it available to help others, you are guilty of hoarding. Oftentimes we think those things are of no value, but they would not be given if there was no purpose for it. God does not create for the fun of it. He looks at a need and provides the solution.

Do you not know you are gods; you are co-creators, and you must live your life creating solutions to problems. You are a solution to the problem in your

51

generation. The problem of staying small is because you have refused to give. You may say, I do not have anything to give like the Shunamite widow in the book of life. She was already depressed and thought she would die with her son. My thought was, even her son did not think he had anything to offer too. She had allowed her negativity to affect her life and her son's life, and she made the decision of hopelessness on their behalf.

Until you let go of what is in your hand, there would be no breakthrough. This does not seem to make any sense, right? But that is one of the natural laws of nature. You get back with the measure you give out. So, what is in your hand, what gold mine are you sitting on, what do you possess others are looking for?

The reality is that we are not as helpless as we think in shaping our lives and destiny. You need to give something out for the universe to give back to you. I have seen a lot of people stuck in the same place because of something for nothing attitude. They are always looking for someone to help them but never make themselves available to be of help to others.

Someone said to me if you are getting free, you are probably the product. All good things come with a price. When you give, you are shifting attention from yourself to others, and it will ultimately give you the highest satisfaction and boost your self-worth and confidence. It is often said that one of the best ways to disperse loneliness and be happy is through volunteering. Using your time and enhancing the lives of others bring great emotional reward

Reflection

Think of all the people in your life who benefited from someone who gave selflessly to a cause and sees how that has helped others live a better life. Imagine all the lives that are touched by the generosity of just one person and imagine if everyone keeps that cycle of giving.

Exercise

Make a list of all the resources in your possession you can use to help humanity. Start by helping at least one person. Give, and it shall be given back to you!

Day 10

Love Makes the Difference

Love is one of the most powerful emotions. The answer to overcoming most life challenges. It is simply impossible to live the ultimate life without loving yourself and others. Great inventions are borne out of the love of solving a need first. If you have a love for others, you go the extra mile of looking for solutions to their problems.

When I talk about love for others, I refer to Agape love – true and pure love. The kind that holds nations, tribes, ethnic groups, and nations together. This type of love is patient, kind, does not envy, boastful, or proud. It does not dishonour others; neither is self-seeking. It is not easily angered and keeps no record of offences. It rejoices in truth, protects, and perseveres. It is trustful, hopeful, and fails not.

Loving yourself is crucial as you cannot love others if you can't love yourself. Can you give what you don't have? It comes with accepting who you are, accepting your shortcomings, and not comparing yourself with others. Self-love plays an important role in every area of your life. It affects your self-image, self–esteem, personal brand, coping capability and how you respond to life challenges in general.

It also comes with certain responsibilities of caring for yourself. It bothers me when I see people drive recklessly on the road endangering others, drink to a state of stupor and sometimes drive, smoke when it is clearly stated that cigarettes can drastically reduce life span and quality, eat what is not good for the body and yet we claim to love us. What quality of life can we have when we are sick in the body? How do we fulfil our life purpose when our life is suddenly cut short through carelessness? We owe it to ourselves, our family, and society to look after ourselves and others in our care to the best of our ability. Life is a gift that must be treasured, don't misuse the privilege

What about harbouring and nurturing negative emotions?

When we harbour negative emotions, we hurt ourselves. The body produces toxins that are harmful to the body, and you are putting more stress on the kidney and liver. Some of these toxins cannot leave the body; they become the little things that disrupt our body functions, like blocked arteries, cancer, emotional breakdown, depression, and anxiety. If you love yourself, you will de-clutter your mind, forgive more and get rid of negative thoughts.

A sick person cannot come to his full potential, and a dead person is buried with all his talents and potentials. He cannot contribute anything to the world. Loving yourself is looking after your body, taking care of your mind and, maintaining a connection with the supreme God, who is the greatest source of love. You can tap into this supreme and pure love by recognising his presence in your life, loving him, and extending that love unto others.

"Because one believes in oneself, one doesn't try to convince others. Because one is content with oneself, one doesn't need others' approval. Because

57

one accepts oneself, the whole world accepts him or her."– Lao-Tzu

Reflection

Take a minute to ponder on this important question- Do you really love yourself? Most people think this is an obvious question, but the truth is- the answer may be NO!

Exercises

List down all the habits and patterns in your life that may be hurting you and others and make that decision to correct them today.

Day 11

Maintain a Positive Attitude

If you don't like something, change it. If you can't change it, change your attitude. - Maya

Attitude refers to the way in which a person thinks or feels and is expressed through his behaviour. Attitude is built up over the years, and hence it is mainly defined by our thoughts carried on through childhood. This attitude becomes a habit over time, and the habits of a person reveal their character. It is said that a positive attitude makes people perform better than the rest. Life is sometimes not about what is happening to you but how you react to it. To become that magnificent person, you must maintain a positive attitude, which will help tide you over difficult periods. We were never promised a life free from obstacles. Things we did not plan will come to obstruct our plans from time to time, but our attitude

59

will determine how we handle these. Our attitude is our predisposition to things, issues, and circumstances.

Since our attitude is an offshoot of our thought, changing our attitude would mean changing our reasoning, which is where the seeds are sown. Your personal effort can get you somewhere, but what keeps you there is your attitude. Your attitude will determine how you react to situations and circumstances. Your attitude will determine your altitude. People may hear your words, but they feel your attitudes. – John C. Maxwell

Are you the type that gives up easily? Do you allow what people do to discourage you? Do you constantly imagine everyone does not like you? Are you quarrelsome? I have worked with people over the years and had an opportunity to work with customers directly, dealing with queries by email and on the phone, and I can tell you a lot of people are not generally happy. If you do not have the right attitude yourself, you will become unhappy dealing with these queries. There are days you want to just curl into a corner after dealing with an angry customer, and it was still early in the morning, another 30 customers to deal with before the close of business. Your attitude will determine how the rest of the day will be.

A lot of people believe that your ability is more important. The fact that you are extremely gifted doesn't mean you will succeed; in fact, I have seen a lot of gifted people not achieving much in life because of their attitude. Different experts have said that if you are able to maintain full concentration and focus combined with a positive attitude, you can surpass a more brilliant competitor who lacks these qualities.

For the testimony of this fact, take this striking quotation from Charles Darwin.

``I have no great quickness of apprehension or wit, which is so remarkable in some clever men," he writes. ``I am a poor critic. . .. My power to follow along and purely abstract train of thought is very limited; and therefore, I never could have succeeded with metaphysics or mathematics. My memory is extensive yet hazy; it suffices to make me cautious by vaguely telling me that I have observed or read something opposed to the conclusion which I am drawing, or on the other hand, in favour of it. So poor in one sense is *my memory that I have never been able to remember a single date or a line of poetry for more than a few days. I have a fair share of the invention and of common sense or judgment, such as every successful lawyer or doctor must-have, but not, I believe, in any higher degree."*

Charles Darwin, despite all these challenges, forged ahead with careless determination to achieve mastery and success. He was not deterred by negative circumstances around him compounded by ill health but worked based on his limited capacity to become renowned for his work on the study of evolution.

I also want to point out that having the right attitude means understanding that life is a personal race and not a competition. We all have something others don't have, and others have what we do not have. Use what you have to the best of your ability to achieve your aim.

One of the common questions I get asked is why do we see a change in attitude when people experience a change in circumstances which may be either negative or positive? A careful study concludes that adversity or fortune does not determine your character, but it only reveals your true self. Different circumstances will reveal a person's true character.

Reflection

Attitude is how we allow circumstances and events around us to affect us, and we have a choice based on the interpretation we give to that event. The fact that you did not get a job does not mean you are not good enough. You are not just a perfect fit for the role. When things don't work in your favour, stay positive and look forward to another time.

Exercises

Think about some undesirable outcomes in the past and how you reacted to them. What was your reaction? Do you think it was positive?

What will a positive reaction to the event look like?

Day 12

Get Back Your Personal Power

We all have personal power, and it is our responsibility to cultivate it and nurture it. When I say personal power here, I do not mean it in a negative like coercion and negative influences over others. Personal power here means the ability to make your own decisions and own them. Not allowing other people's beliefs and actions to dictate the course of your life. It is recognising your abilities and not concentrating on things you do not do so well.

People often think you only have power when you assume powerful roles, but personal power cannot be gifted- it is innate. The trick is to connect with it and own it. To live the ultimate life, you must own your personal power. This allows you to stand up for yourself; you move from the position of the victim to become a master over your life. It helps you build confidence as people start to trust you more. Regaining your personal power helps build your resilience and emotional mastery.

Personal power is more about self-realisation and self-mastery. It is more an attitude or state of mind and is not geared toward control of others and should not be confused with other types of power. It is based on competence, vision, positive personal qualities, and service. It is more generous, creative, and humane when compared to other forms of power.

Also, there is a covert negative power that we need to watch out for as this may have subtle but profoundly influences the use of our personal power. This type is based on a passive form of aggression. This is very common among friends and families and needs to be mentioned. I have seen this so often in coaching sessions, and people are unaware they are being manipulated because it is so subtle.

This type can manifest when someone refuses to take responsibility for their own actions but make others, such as family members, accountable for their misery and unhappiness. Often these people manipulate their victims by arousing in them feelings of guilt, fear and anger and often play the victim. For example, abusive spouses often threaten to kill themselves or their victims if the other threatens to leave them. People who lead chronically addictive lifestyles or are self-destructive can threaten suicide as a way of eliciting fear in their loved ones. These are a few examples. The important thing you need to watch out for are actions from others that rob you of your personal power. Understand that you are not the cause of their misery or whatever they are going through. Offer to support them as best as you can but don't blame yourself for the outcomes in their lives.

How to gain personal power

There are different ways of gaining personal power, but I will mention five in this chapter.

1) Set boundaries- This is very important as this allows us and others to understand what we do and don't do. It is not just enough for us to understand our boundaries but let others know as well. There is a popular saying- let your "yes be a yes, and your no be a no". It may be difficult for people to accept this at first if it is not in their

favour, but they will eventually respect your wish.

2) Get out of the victim mode- A friend once told me after I described very upsetting incidents – he said anyone who has the power to upset you this much has power over your life. You are not responsible for what others do to you, but you are responsible for your response and actions.

   Two things you can do, you can either get out of the relationship or change how you respond to the upsetting behaviours. And this brings me to the next point.

3) Watch out for toxic people- It is very difficult to manage toxic relationships, especially where it involves people who are not willing to change their behaviours. Trying to manage these relationships often leave us depleted and strip us of our personal power. Some relationships are not meant to last. Once you have tried your best, evaluate things and if you are unhappy- consider moving on. The people you relate with will have an impact on your destiny. It isn't

68

something to gloss over, as some relationships can terminate your very existence.

4) Commit to your values- Know what is important and not important and be true to yourself. Live your life not subject to people's approval but stay true and in tune with your personal values.

5) Learn self-compassion- We find it easy to forgive others sometimes but can't forgive ourselves. If you make a mistake, learn from it, and move on and don't penalise yourself forever.

Refection

Think about events, circumstances or people that are constantly draining your energy and how you can reverse that. Remember, your personal power is yours, and you don't need permission to own it.

Exercises

List the three things you want to do to take charge of your life and gain your power back.

Day 13

Character As a Superpower

One great influence we have, which we sometimes don't think about, is our personal influence. We may think setting out to impress people outwardly is the ultimate, but the power of the subconscious influence is even greater, that silent and subtle radiation of our character over time. The effect of our words and actions and all those things we do unconsciously may either bring people closer or push them away from us.

Now let us consider these three words, personality, character, and charisma.

While we may think our character is the same as our personality, they are different. The main difference between our character and personality is that it is easy to make out one's personality at the first meeting. Still, your character is not easy to determine immediately. Your character is who you are on the inside, and your personality is on the outside. Character refers to the mental and moral qualities an individual possesses that distinguish them from others-these qualities have a moral compass of either good or bad. The traits of personality are personal and physical.

Character is also different from charisma- while the character is the totality of who you are, the way we act when no one is looking. Charisma is the ability to elicit favour in people. It is having power over others.

Our character will always remain with us even after we have left this world, as people would still refer to our character after we depart this world, either good or bad. It is the superpower we possess because we may impress people in a short time, but our character will eventually evolve and, if found wanting, could destroy all our efforts and hard work.

There are different kinds of people based on their character. There are people whose presence seems to radiate sunshine, cheer and optimism and you feel constantly calmed and restored when they are around you. On the other hand, some people move around like icebergs; they are cold, reserved, unapproachable and totally immersed in their world. People want to avoid these people. There are the argumentative, troublesome people who seem to be angry at life and pick at everything directed at them. What about the oversensitive people who avoid everyone and can't bear to hear the truth?

Some can't be trusted and are insincere in the heart. They will show connection and attachment to you only when they need you and bring out their best smile, but nobody is fooled as people are able to see through the façade because we have in us the power of intuition to sense and warn us not to trust certain people. And then, the unserious ones will not only waste their time but also want to waste other people's time.

To be truly magnificent, you need to build your character. You are choosing to do the right thing, which may sometimes be difficult. There is an African proverb that says, "A good name is better than silver and gold" Your character has a great influence on your identity as it influences how people perceive you. As the character is derived from a chisel, it means it does not happen by itself; Our character is a conscious choice of design. You can choose to be good or bad, honest, or dishonest, kind, or rude, and the list goes on. It is ultimately our choice.

You may feel discouraged that when you try to live right as it seems, you don't make an awful lot of impact but living the ultimate life is not about living a dishonest life. One of the ways people of faith are distinguished is through the fruits of the spirit "By their fruits; we shall know them" If you say you are magnificent, you must exhibit a good character. It is not enough to say you are magnificent when you cannot be a person of integrity.

To make our influence felt, we must live by faith and be a role model. When you say to people don't lie, you should not be lying. A magnet does not attract iron as iron. It must first convert the iron into another magnet before it can attract it. We should not sacrifice love and compassion for humanity in our quest for success; we must see influence through the filter of human love and sympathy. We should not merely be an influencer but an inspiration and tower of strength to others.

Reflection

Our character is who we truly are. Even when we deceive others, should we lie to ourselves? Think about the list of good and bad traits you have.

Exercise

Write down all your good and bad traits

Ask yourself why they are there

Circle all the bad traits you have and reflect on what is reinforcing them

What can you do to change them? Write these down

Day 14

The Source of Infinite Power

We have read about our thoughts in the previous chapters as one of the greatest sources of power available to us. We also read that the mind connects the spiritual to the physical. Now let us look at the power of the spiritual man.

There is a potential infinite power available to us we often are not aware of, and it is the power of the spirit. With this power, things that you think are impossible can become possible. This Power of the Spirit is unconquerable- It is not the power of ordinary life, finite will, or the human mind. It transcends these because being spiritual; it is of a higher order than either physical or even mental. You can only come to the fullness of this power when you become awakened and tap into its divine source.

If you do not believe that God exists, you cannot tap into that power. If you believe that a human is merely a physical being, then you will operate under the limited power of the physical, and if, on the other hand, you believe humans are spiritual beings, then you are able to possess all the powers of a spiritual being. What you choose to believe is entirely up to you. You may think we evolved through time, and there is no God that is fine, and you can choose to believe there is a God, the source of infinite power, and tap into his strength. As one who has seen and enjoyed the power of God multiple times in profound ways, I think it would not be fair if I did not mention this in the book. While I may not dwell so much on this much, but I want you to be awakened in your spirit of this power and seek it to come to the fullness of your glory.

We are gods because we are made in his image and likeness. We are also created by him and for his purpose. Which means we must acknowledge him and serve him. When we connect to this divine source through the holy spirit, we can know the mind of God, and we will have revelation knowledge of things to come.

While our thought can be likened to the spiritual power of tremendous potency, it is not the same as our spiritual power. Through our minds, we can either connect or alienate ourselves from the divine power of God. We connect to God through faith. We cannot know God unless we believe he exists and reward those who diligently seek him.

The truth is that we have never been truly separated from our divine source. The separation is merely mental through blindness and unbelief. How can we be separated from our spiritual source when we are spirit beings ourselves? It is in Him we live, move, and have our being. As soon as we realise our relationship to the Infinite, we move from a zone of weakness to power, from death unto life. One moment we feel alone, far weak, and we suddenly realise we are nothing less than a son of God, and we can draw unto that power of the infinite that comes with all a son's privileges.

To connect to the source of divine power and enter our inheritance, A change must take place. We must learn to think after the Spirit as a spiritual being instead of after the flesh- as a material creature. Just like the prodigal son in the book of life, who had to come to himself and leave the husks and the swine in the far country, returning to his father's house, where there is bread of life. To learn to think after the spirit, we must learn to communicate through prayer to God, read his words and seek him daily.

Reflection

Think about drawing unto a greater source of power than you already possess and how that will make a huge difference in your life.

Exercises

If you want to draw that strength to you, just declare the following:

Oh God, I want you to reveal yourself to me as the source of infinite power. - Do this continuously until God reveals himself to you.

Day 15

Your Daily Habits Matter

A lot has been said about the power of our minds -thoughts which are produced in mind as powerful tools to achieve our ultimate life dreams. Even though these thoughts are powerful, if this is not backed by action, it is useless - Just like faith without works is dead.

Having established this, this brings us to a very important aspect of our life, our daily habits. Our habits, in simple terms, are things we practice regularly, especially the ones we find difficult to give up. We have heard several times that humans are creatures of habit. We tend to settle into similar routines over time. For example, I wake up about the same time every day without any alarm, irrespective of when I go to bed. My morning routine is so important to me as it sets the tone for the day, and I usually stick with it unless it is necessary to break it. The secret to our success is revealed in our daily routines. No matter how grand our goals look, there is simply no use if we don't stick with the plans. We can always find something to do to occupy each day, but the question is, are we working in the direction of our goal?

Many people have habits that are not beneficial to them and desire to change this. However, people are doing it the wrong way. It is often said you need twenty-one days to change a habit, and this has been reviewed again, and different suggestions were made, but the average is now about sixty-six days to develop a new set of habits. Changing a habit may be successful or not, depending on your approach.

You can't hope to change your habit by fighting it, as the more you do this, the stronger they become. We give power to what we focus on, and they become stronger; we need to develop a new one to replace the bad habit and consistently practise it until it becomes an established habit.

In changing a particular bad habit, often people want to use autosuggestion to replace and get rid of their bad habit, but the right action must accompany this to be successful. The power that produces the habits is the same in each case; it is the way in which this power is directed that is essential. Initially, it may be difficult to divert the mind away from a particular thought that produces a habit, but as the habit is repeated over time, it becomes ingrained in the brain and nervous system. The new ones will replace the cells formerly used for wrong thinking – new pathways are produced.

When you settle into a new habit, it is also important to maintain it. The fact that you established a habit of exercising does not mean you can't reverse it if you stop exercising. For example, that is why a crash diet is not recommended, but making healthy choices as a way of life.

Another thing I hear people struggle with is the motivation to act, and they find themselves struggling to make changes in their lives. One way to deal with this is to make little changes at a time. Let us assume we want to start a new habit of reading daily, which is fantastic, by the way. Don't start with the fifty pages a day; you can start with just ten pages and move it up gradually. Also, make sure you reduce any form of friction- if, for example, you are an auditory learner, you might want to get an audiobook instead.

Another thing you can do is to tie down a new habit to some established habits like listening to a book while driving to work since you already drive to work anyway. You can also benefit from a network of friends, groups or people who also want to make the same changes as you—providing some form of support and accountability to each other.

Reflection

Think about how changing your habits can affect your life, especially over a long time, and determine to change all negative habits in your life holding you back. Have a picture of the ultimate life you desire to serve as motivation.

Exercise

Make a list of all the things you do daily on the left-hand side. And on the right, list everything in your life that happens automatically. Provide details as much as possible. Then try and tie a new habit to possible triggers on the list.

Example:

I have tea breaks as part of my daily routine, which has been established over time. Now, I want to start a new habit of stretching in between work to improve my circulation. I decided to tie a two-minute stretch to my tea breaks to establish a pattern.

Day 16

Motivation and Willpower

There are numerous articles, books, and theories on motivations. This is because motivation has a huge effect on performance. Motivation is the reason we act or do something. Organisations spend millions on resources to keep staff motivated. Athletes are constantly motivated to achieve outstanding results. Students are kept motivated to achieve academic excellence! To become truly magnificent, you need the motivation to do all that is required for your goal attainment. If you do not desire to do something, it would be very difficult to achieve great results.

One question I am constantly asked is how do I motivate myself to start a new course of desirable action? The willingness is obviously there, but something is hindering you from starting. One way to deal with a lack of motivation is just to act- just do it. Don't wait until you feel like it. Once you start, you gain momentum, and this causes you to continue as the feel-good hormone is released after you achieve some results. A lot of times, we look for excuses not to start. Instead, look for a reason to start as perfect circumstances does not exist.

Another way to overcome a lack of motivation is to develop a strong why? If your reason for starting something is not strong enough, it is so easy to fall behind in developing a strong why as emotional connection to that goal comes into play. I had this vision of helping the less privileged people in Africa and started an organisation for this purpose called Pathways International Mission- an organisation devoted to poverty eradication and inequality. This idea was born from watching a documentary where mud flakes were fed to children. - Mud flakes are made from mud which is sieved to remove the stones. The children and their mothers were so hungry that the mothers had to stuff their tummies with mud! I cried so much that morning because I was just recovering from emotional trauma and had thought my situation was the most difficult. On my plate were two pieces of chicken and a large bowl of cereal. Anytime I felt like quitting, that image comes back to me to remind me of my reason for starting in the first place.

Another concept that is closely tied to motivation is the concept of Will Power. Sometimes it is not about starting but how not to quit. While motivation keeps you acting, willpower works in the opposite direction- it is responsible for quitting. When you walk into a room full of pastries and if you have a sudden instinct to grab the cakes and you did. That is your willpower! According to a definition of willpower by psychologists, "willpower is the ability to delay gratification and resist short-term temptations to meet long-term goals". Our will power the ability to exercise restraint and self-discipline. If you cannot exercise self-control and discipline, you cannot live your ultimate life and become the magnificent person you are created to be. It is convenient to take the easy route, and that is why it is easy in the first place. Treasures are not found on the surface; you dig deep, and after that, it is passed through fire for refining. The price for success is something a lot of people are not willing to pay. It takes discipline, hard work and commitment.

Self-Discipline makes you commit to whatever goal you have set in place for yourself. At any point in time, we have choices to make. Eat or not, sleep or not, work or play. Study or watch movies. It is the correct application of your willpower that makes you take the right decision at any point in time. Willpower is like a muscle, and the more you use it, the more it stretches. The way to develop your willpower is to do the exact opposite of what you wish to do.

You can do other things to increase motivation – you can link the event you are struggling with to some other things in your life you already enjoy. As an example, I enjoy my walks in the morning because I listen to my favourite songs while on the walk. You can also reward yourself after successfully completing a task as this reinforces the positive behaviour and keeps you motivated. Don't wait until the big picture is completed; make it a daily habit of rewarding yourself.

Meditation also helps with motivation and willpower as it helps with focus. Meditation is nothing mystical; it is all about focusing the mind and taking control of your attention. When you meditate, you practise clearing the mind of distracting thoughts and focusing on nothing.

Reflection

Think about a project you completed successfully; this shows you have the power to achieve anything you want, and you can always draw on to that power at will. You are in absolute control!

Exercises

List all the goals you want to achieve and ask yourself why you want to achieve them.

Develop a picture of what achieving the goals will look like to keep you motivated.

Day 17

Let Go of The Past

B rothers, I do not consider myself yet to have taken hold of it. But one thing I do: Forgetting what is behind and straining toward what is ahead." Philippians 3:13

To become truly magnificent, you must learn to put the past behind you. If you constantly dwell in your past, it is difficult to move forward—it is like driving a car and facing backwards. I have observed that inability to let go is one of the main challenges people face during coaching sessions involving relationship issues. This becomes a cankerworm that spreads to other areas of life if left unchecked. When you are constantly reliving the past, it is difficult to live in the moment. Nothing that happened in the past can be changed, but you can learn from your experiences and move on.

In dealing with the past, you will need to be honest with yourself, look at things from all angles and see what could be done differently. What went wrong and why? That assessment is essential to evaluate things and put them in their proper perspective, but it should be for that purpose only- No blame games.

Forgiveness is an essential part of dealing with the past. All of us have dealt with deep hurts from our past that still negatively influence our lives. Without practising forgiveness, our hurts become like deep wounds that won't heal. Forgiving a grievance, whether real or imagined, is one of the best gifts you can give yourself, irrespective of whether the person deserves it or not. When we refuse to forgive, we become resentful. Holding on to resentment is like drinking poison and expecting the person causing us pain to suffer. Sometimes the people that hurt us are not even aware of it. They are living freely and happy, but we are killing ourselves slowly when we harbour hatred and resentment in our lives.

Resentment is a negative emotion, and we must get rid of it if we are to move ahead. Forgiving people empowers us. It means we are stronger in character and gives us an advantage over others. Resentment is that little thing that can hinder our growth and success. Imagine a tiny insect inside our eyes, irritating and disturbing. It clogs our vision, and until we get rid of it, we cannot move forward. Resentment can easily become hate, and hatred is a very strong negative emotion.

Resentment can cause both physical and emotional illness because of the toxins released into the body. It takes up so much energy and affects our ability to focus. It compromises our immune system, and one of the exercises for healing cancer patients is by encouraging them to forgive. In my personal battle with emotional trauma, it was an integral part of my healing process. Forgiveness is not only about forgiving others but forgiving ourselves also for past mistakes.

I talked to someone about forgiveness, and she asked if forgiveness means blotting out the incident like it never occurred. Absolutely not, you will still have a recollection of the event, but you change your thoughts around the situation or person that caused the pain to a positive one. Release them from your mind and take a deep breath. A lot of times, it is better to deal with issues straight away and not let them escalate. If someone is hurting you, let them know before things get out of hand, as they may not even be aware. Forgiving others is hard; it takes emotional strength and will, and love. Love is said to cover a multitude of sins!

"The weak can never forgive. Forgiveness is the attribute of the strong."- Gandhi

Reflection

It is generally agreed that forgiveness is a deliberate decision to release feelings of resentment or vengeance which are directed at persons or groups. It does not matter who is right or wrong or whether they deserve to be forgiven or not. Forgiveness is empowering; it is liberating and brings a sense of inner peace. It does not free the other person from liability of the offence, nor does it mean you forgot what happened either. It is just a conscious decision of moving on and shedding the baggage of hurt and resentment.

Exercise

Write down the names of those who have hurt you and what they did.

Write down their qualities, and what they have done in the past that was beneficial.

Determine to strike out their faults and replace these with their good qualities.

Day 18

Work Hard and Smart

"Nothing ever comes to one that is worth having, except as a result of hard work". Booker T. Washington

I was in the labour room having my second child 19 years ago. It was a long, arduous labour, not progressing, and I was about to be sent back home. I knew it was not the case of false labour, and I had to do something. I managed to convince the doctor to allow me to stay till morning, and if nothing happens, I can be discharged. To improve my chance of having the baby, I did not just lie down in the ward; I walked around the whole place despite the fact I was in pain. At a point during the delivery, I could not continue and told the doctor; this is so hard- he said, yes, it is hard- that is why it is called labour. To birth your dreams, you may need to push harder than before, work harder than before, go the extra mile than you did before.

Creating that ultimate life, you desire won't manifest by wishful thinking and planning. Anyone that is diligent at work will stand out from others. While nature provides the raw material, we make the finished products. You don't only need to work hard but also work smart. I have seen people go through work in reverse order. Work processes need to be planned in an efficient yet effective way to manage time and resources. Educate yourself to learn tips and tricks to accomplish goals faster.

Working smarter does not mean you will not work hard; there is no bypassing that, but it is a more effective way of working. One of the things I do which helped me a great deal is that I ask questions. I am neither ashamed nor afraid to ask people to teach me things. I sometimes try to figure things out myself, but I often reach out to people who have already completed the task so many times before me, and before you know it, I am flying through the task. Working smart also means you are completing tasks that are important to realising your dreams. Don't just be busy being busy. There are tasks that are important but not urgent. You can also delegate tasks; you don't have to be a jack of all trades. If you are not good in some areas, you can find someone to do it for much less time because time is costly!

Hard work doesn't just mean the hours you spend trying to achieve your goals. Remaining mentally focused and alert takes sheer determination and hard work itself. There will be times that you veer off course. But this is all part of your learning curve. The only way you can avoid making mistakes and keep on track along the way is by trial and error. This invariably means that you should not get discouraged when you do not get it right at the initial stages. Let's consider Thomas Edison, the man who discovered the light bulb. It took him 1000 attempts to invent the light bulb, and each one failed until the 1001 attempt. Now that's hard work! Getting knocked back or failing a few times is hard to cope with, but 1000 times really does take some determination to get over it. Edison said that for every failure he had, he simply worked harder until he achieved his goal. And luckily for us, he did!

I remember listening to Mountain of Fire and Miracles Ministries' general overseer, one of the biggest churches in Nigeria with branches worldwide. He mentioned he does not get more than five hours of sleep every day. In fact, by his standard, that is too much; it is no wonder he can accomplish so much in his personal and spiritual life. It is true that positive thinking and clear goals will help you; hard work goes hand in hand towards building your dream life.

There are no quick fixes to success; work is required. I am not an advocate of getting rich quick scheme. I strongly believe that if it looks too good to be true, it probably is too good to be true. If it was so easy, everyone would be doing it.

Ken Poirot said, "Hard work increases the probability of serendipity." Serendipity is the act of finding something unexpected when you are least expecting it. In other words, along with hard work come rewards, sometimes a reward you didn't think would occur. I have seen people who are talented and hard workers recommended for opportunities without applying for them.

Working hard and smart also means you can set priorities, manage distractions from family and friends, and get enough rest. Don't work yourself to death! People who work harder than others are suddenly rewarded, and people think they are just lucky. Luck is just where opportunity meets preparation. The initial work would have been done first.

"Success is the result of perfection, hard work, learning from failure, loyalty, and persistence." – Colin Powell

Reflection

It is important to work hard and work smarter as you have only twenty-four hours in a day like others. Think about times when you think you could have completed some tasks in a more efficient yet effective way.

Exercises

List your daily tasks and see what part of them you can delegate and the ones you can find a more effective way of completing.

Day 19

Be Committed and Persistent

"Freedom is not the absence of commitments, but the ability to choose - and commit myself to - what is best for me." – Paulo Coelho, The Zahir

In the previous chapter, we talked about hard work associated with acting on our goals. Great ideas not backed by action is nothing. It is also important to note that not only do you need to act, but you need to be committed, consistent and persistent.

Commitment means you dedicate time and effort to your goals. To get tangible results, you don't only need to be committed but be consistent as well. You need to execute tasks based on a routine and stick with it, albeit with all the distractions. Creating the ultimate life requires you to honour these commitments like our lives depend on them. Successful people make a daily habit of what unsuccessful people practice at will. A lot of the problems people have is not about making commitments but honouring them. It is easy to say I want to lose weight; it is another thing entirely to commit to a change of lifestyle consistently. While we know that the key to living a successful life is embedded in our daily routine, what makes it difficult for us to make the right choices? The answer is simple; it is difficult to commit to a particular thing. It takes effort, discipline and removing all necessary distractions. One of the benefits of commitment is that you master tasks quickly because you are doing them regularly at regular times and intervals, and it becomes a part of us.

Be Persistent

"Nothing in this world can take the place of persistence. Talent will not; nothing is more common than unsuccessful men with talent. Genius will not; unrewarded genius is almost a proverb. Education will not; the world is full of educated derelicts. Persistence and determination alone are omnipotent. The slogan Press On! Has solved and always will solve the problems of humans." – Calvin Coolidge

The ability to persist in the face of opposition and roadblock is essential. A persistent person gets results when others have given up. Persistence means not giving up, having a strong resolve, unwavering in the face of opposition. When you are persistent, you are a person who is determined to keep trying at things without minding the obstacles. I remember an incident clearly when I went to my son's school for a parent-teacher meeting. The teacher told me; your son got on the debating team even though he was not recommended. I was suddenly interested, and so I asked the obvious question. How did he convince you? She answered, he waited for a week for me after each class to remind me he was still interested in joining the debating team, and after a week, I could not help but yield to his request.

The lives of successful people are characterised by their ability to persist in the face of opposition, Disregarding people's opinions, defying obstacles, and protocols, breaking the rules and demolishing the status quo.

Michael Jordan, the famous basketball player, was quoted to have said this about himself.

"I've missed more than 9000 shots in my career.

I've lost almost 300 games

Twenty-six times I've been trusted to take the game-winning shot ... and missed.

I've failed over and over and over again in my life. That is why I succeed."

~ Michael Jordan

Perhaps, I would say I find the story of Abraham Lincoln as one of the greatest examples of persistence. He was born into a poor family and repeatedly failed throughout his life. Lincoln was a champion who did not give up. He had so many reasons to give up from the loss of his home, business, job, money, and wife. He also suffered numerous defeats and had a nervous breakdown. He nonetheless persisted to become the president of the United States of America.

"A river cuts through rock, not because of its power, but because of its persistence." —James N. Watkins.

Refection

Think about what you succeeded at and the obstacles you faced. How many times have you been frustrated and wanted to give up? Now tap into that strength for something you want to achieve now and determine you will not give up until you win.

Exercise

Write down three things you can do to remove distractions and increase your focus and commitment.

Day 20

Power of Focus

"The successful warrior is the average man with a laser-like focus"- Bruce Lee

Everyone who made notable success had something in common- they all possess a laser-like focus—doing only one thing at a time and concentrating all their efforts on it. The ultimate life requires a purpose, vision, and goal, which we already talked about. In addition, it involves directing all energy into that one thing you want. So many people start their journey to magnificence with a lot of enthusiasm, preparation, and passion, but along the way, they are side-tracked by other ideas, life events or general life distractions. They start off with a good idea, also possessing everything else to make it work but lacking the ability to focus. They lack the ability to concentrate on one thing at a time amidst distractions and criticism. They are not able to obliterate other ideas and isolate one main idea and follow it through to completion. A soon as they start from one project, they are distracted by another brilliant idea they also wish to take on. There are so many good ideas, but you cannot do everything at the same time and get great results

The man with concentration, or the power of continued enthusiastic application, will surpass a brilliant competitor if the latter is careless and indifferent towards his work. Many who have accomplished great things in business in their professional lives would understand that the connection between the body and the mind is intimate.

The body needs to be functioning optimally for the mind to function well, and likewise, the mind needs to be functioning optimally for the body to work perfectly well. The power of concentration is thus affected by a lot of factors such as good sleep, quality of food you eat, your rest, your relationships and your total outlook on life, and the perfect working of the body is necessary to the highest efficiency of the mind.

In maintaining focus, you must also regulate how mental energy is dissipated. Anger and strong emotions have a way of draining energy. Be sure that you are well relaxed, not under any pressure but consistently maintaining your focus on the assignment before you. Your mental energy should be channelled to the right source.

If you can point to a man who has different projects simultaneously, then I can show you a man who is not ready to create their ultimate life. When you shoot, it must be targeted. If you fail to direct your mental energies through focusing on a thing, the result is a dissipated effort. You do not gain mastery in anything. Like they say, Jack of all trade- master of none!

Mental energy, if not checked, can become diffusive, and that is why there is always a pull to start different things as soon as it catches your fancy. However, the lure is, you must resist, stand your ground, and focus on one thing at a time. You must learn to direct and control your own mental energies and that of others as well. This will mean understanding the emotions of others and learning how to direct them. There isn't a problem with having different ideas but working with one idea at a time. Give it time for it to be nurtured and grow. In your career or business transformation quest, it is important you gain self-mastery and control.

Failure to do this will lead to constantly being engaged in things that do not promote the growth of your business or enhance your career. You can be very busy, but if such efforts are not targeted, they will not produce the results you require in the shortest possible time.

"I don't care how much power, brilliance or energy you have; if you don't harness it and focus it on a specific target and hold it there, you're never going to accomplish as much as your ability warrants." Zig Ziglar

Reflection

Whatever you focus on takes your energy. Make sure you are channelling your energy on the right things and take projects one at a time.

Exercise

Identify things in your life that might be draining your energies. Also, identify how you want to deal with these.

Day 21

Health is Wealth

L ooking after our health is an integral part of living the ultimate life. It only makes sense that you make sure you are alive to see your dreams materialise. Once we are dead, all the big dreams, visions, and ideas we have are buried with us. Unfortunately, there is no opportunity for a second chance in the grave, and that is why we must make this one experience count -Enjoying each day and making the best out of it. We have learned about the interconnectedness of the mind and the body. It means that we must not only look after our physical body but also our mind.

"Health is harmony—a delicate balance and adjustment between spirit, soul, mind, and body."-Unknown

Your health impacts directly on your mood, your ability to complete physically or mentally demanding tasks and even your looks. If you are not in good health, you will struggle to complete your daily goals. Imagine falling sick during an examination; even if you are the most brilliant in the class, it will adversely affect your performance.

Looking after one's health should not be difficult these days as there is a huge amount of online and offline resources, but I am just going to mention a few things we can do to ensure we stay healthy. One thing we do that needs to be pointed out is that when it comes to health, care needs to be taken, and self-medication is not advised. Any concern about your health should be discussed with your doctor. There are people on medication for certain ailments; these people should always check with their doctor before embarking on any diet or exercise programs.

Often, we treat the symptoms, and the root cause of an illness is not dealt with. When there is pain or problem in a part of the body- it is a way, our body tells us to pay attention. At the onset of the covid crisis, I remember that we started to work from home, and the only thing we did was to shop for groceries and food items. I noticed I started to feel pains in my chest, and at a point, I thought I had caught the virus. I later realised it was because of a lack of exercise and a change in diet, which was not healthy. As soon as I changed my diet and lost some weight, all the symptoms disappeared.

Diet - Looking after our health means we eat the right nutrients needed by the body and mind to function properly in the right amount and quantity based on our age, body type, height, and lifestyle. It means you must understand your needs and requirements properly. I have often heard people say we are what we eat. This is so true because our food is the fuel required for the body to function well. We need food as a source of energy to fuel the cells in our bodies. Vitamin D, the sunshine vitamin, is the precursor for major hormones in our body. Vitamin C is required for immunity and stress reduction. Magnesium helps form bone and connective tissue by helping with the uptake of calcium. It prevents muscle pains and aches, accelerates learning through brain plasticity, enhances our sleep, etc. The B vitamins are required for a healthy nervous system. This is to list a few. Imagine if we are deficient in these essential minerals and vitamins, it would be difficult for the body to function optimally. In essence, we need to change how we think about food. We eat to live, and we do not live to eat.

I do not advocate crash diet programs even though we know the danger of obesity; I believe in a lifestyle change instead. Moderation is the key. I was discussing with a client who was gaining weight, and she mentioned she had been eating right. So, we took an inventory of what she consumed that week and realised she had large portions of oranges and bananas, and this was triggering her weight gain. The point I am making is even foods that are considered healthy should be consumed in moderation. If we can apply self-discipline and moderation to most things, our life will be much better. Anyone battling any form of illness must also banish hatred, anger, resentment, envy, bitterness from their lives because no matter how healthy their diet is, these emotions are negative and may compromise their immune system allowing diseases to flourish.

Exercise- Our body is not designed to sleep and sit all day. It is for movement, and if we sit all day at work and don't exercise, our body will not function well. Taking at least 20 minutes of brisk walk can help take care of this. You can burn a huge number of additional calories by walking to and from work or just getting off your bus a stop later. This will burn calories and help you increase your physical fitness and resting heart rate, and your chances of developing cardiovascular and other serious health-related issues are reduced.

Sleep- This is so important to allow the body and mind to rest. If the mind is disturbed, the quality of sleep is also affected. It is not sometimes how long it is but how well. You can sleep for 5 hours and feel invigorated but also sleep ten hours but feel you have not slept at all. We should make sure we are getting enough quality sleep as required by our bodies.

Drink plenty of water -Recent studies suggest that swapping all your drinks for water can make huge differences to your energy levels, your weight loss and even your mental focus. The reason for this is not only that you'll be putting fewer empty calories into your body, but also that you'll be increasing your metabolism to burn fat at a faster and more efficient rate.

Meditation and Mindfulness – which are often ignored, is a way of restoring balance in the body. They are both very beneficial to health. Meditating daily helps with mental alertness, focus and energy. We will be talking about mindfulness in another chapter.

Reflection

Think about all the consequences of suddenly falling ill and reflect on what this would mean to you, your family, friends, and your community. Is there something you think you can improve on to ensure you stay in good health?

Exercises

List all the lifestyle changes you wish to make and use SMART goals; draw out how you want to achieve this.

Day 22

Master Your Emotions

Every day I hear people ask these questions? Can I truly be happy? Can I truly be fulfilled? Why am I always angry with myself and my situation? Why can't I get out of this depressing situation? Why do I find it difficult to forgive people and move on? Why can't I get along with people? What is this guilt I feel, and why won't it go away? The answer to these questions and many more lies in how we manage our emotions. Our emotions can make us or break us, depending on how it is managed. I could give you too many examples of people who destroyed themselves and others due to lack or improper management of their emotions. It may take you years to build a reputation, but it takes a minute to destroy all of that.

In recent years, the field of emotional intelligence has grown rapidly as more researchers are drawn into that special field that deals with understanding our emotions and other people's emotions. You must understand your own emotions and others, as this will enable you to understand their perspectives and develop empathy. At the core of what we consider right or wrong is our personal value or judgement. It is how we see the world through our lens!

What are Emotions?

Emotions are our reactions to people, events, and circumstances around us and are different from our moods. Emotions are usually of a shorter duration in comparison to our moods. For example, it may be very intense when you are angry, but it usually subsides not too long after. However, moods are less intense but of longer duration than emotions. Also, emotions are directed at people or things, but moods may not be directed at people or events. When you, however, focus on the object or subject of your emotion, this will certainly affect your mood.

Why emotions are important

Internal guidance: Our emotions are there to provide an internal guide. It will alert us when a particular need is not met. For example, when someone feels unloved or unhappy. This may signal a need to connect.

It helps us make decisions: We may decide to go ahead with something if we have a good feeling about it or vice versa.

It helps us define our limits: Our emotions will help us declare boundaries, especially with people. You can easily tell people when they have stepped out of the boundary.

Communication: It helps in our communication with people. When you smile, they know you are comfortable with what is being said and when you are angry, they may quickly apologise, knowing you do not find the conversation pleasing.

It helps us determine our values: The only way we can understand what is important to us is from the feelings we get from it. The things that make us happy are generally things we attach value to.

Bonding: Our emotions have proved very useful in bringing people together and creating a bond. There is a general tendency to hang with people you are happy around and stay away from people who upset you.

Why we should manage our emotions

To become more productive: it is important to manage negative emotions as this can hinder productivity. Emotions of sadness, anxiety and anger are energy drainers.

For better interpersonal relationships: managing your emotions will help you become better at relating better with others.

For greater achievements: If you understand what motivates you, you can always use it as a trigger to stay on course and vice versa; if you know things that upset you, you know how to avoid them when necessary.

It will also help you in avoiding self-sabotage which will be discussed later.

Different types of emotions

There are different kinds of emotions as there are different philosophers and theorists, but for the purpose of this book, we will only discuss our basic emotions. According to Paul Ekman, our basic emotions are anger, disgust, fear, happiness, sadness, and surprise. The next two chapters will be devoted to the management of 4 out of these 6 basic emotions.

Reflection

Understanding our emotions is part of understanding ourselves, and that is just one part of the whole. In addition, we must understand other people's emotions, and it is referred to as emotional intelligence. There are so many benefits attributable to this.

Exercise

Write down all the different emotions you feel for the next one week starting from today to see which is the most frequent and why?

Day 23

The Emotion of Anger and Fear

Anger

Anger is a negative emotion that must be properly managed. It isn't to say you cannot be angry at all but getting angry all the time at the slightest provocation isn't healthy. Also, how you behave and what you do at the time you are angry will guide you on whether the anger has become a challenge. Anger could sabotage your growth effort, and the key to dealing with it is first to understand the type of anger. When channelled correctly and expressed appropriately, anger can help people see the importance of an issue and come to the realisation that corrective action needs to be taken.

Behavioural Anger:

People who experience this type of anger are often confrontational and violent. They will become aggressive and rude, and it has nothing to do with whether the object of their anger is doing something wrong. The issue is with their interpretation of the event. The confrontation may start as verbal abuse, and if the other party is not subdued, it results in violence. This type of anger often requires professional help.

Retaliatory Anger

This is probably the most common. It typically is a result of lashing back at someone who hurt or offended you in a way. You may decide to take it further to a higher level to deter the other person from repeating what happened. It is better to try and resolve issues amicably with dialogue rather than try to even out the score. Two wrongs do not make things right. Communicate with the other person to see how things can be resolved.

Self-Inflicted Anger

This type of anger may result from a feeling of guilt that isn't justified. People use this type of anger to punish themselves for something they think they've done wrong. They may inflict physical pains on themselves as punishment, like cutting themselves, starving themselves. If you find yourself in this situation, quickly seek professional help.

Overwhelming Anger

When anger is overwhelming, it could be because it has been bottled up for so long, and it suddenly erupts. Some may even resort to physical violence and may cause harm to themselves and others. When anger is tending toward violence, professional help must be sought.

Passive Anger

This type of anger is typically non-confrontational and uses avoidance and evasive techniques. It may involve staying away from the object of anger. This is quite common and could be potentially unhealthy.

How to manage anger

According to Thomas Paine, a philosopher, the best way to manage anger is to delay action or reaction. If you feel your anger rising within you, take a moment to calm down before you do something you may regret. Move away from the situation if you can. Use a self-talk technique to regain control of your emotions, e.g., "*Calm down*", "*Relax*". This should be repeated several times. Taking a walk can also help. If none of this help, seek professional help. Anger could be self-destructive if not properly managed.

The Emotions of Fear

Fear, like all other emotions, is natural, and it is there to warn us from danger. It is generally a feeling of anxiety caused by what we think may happen. Experts say 95% of the time, what we fear don't happen. Fear has held a lot of people in one place. Fear is an emotion that must be understood and properly managed to live the ultimate life. Fear can become destructive and debilitating when it isn't controlled. Fear is judged as rational and irrational; an irrational fear is also called phobia.

There are different types of fear, but experts say that there are basically five types of fear

The fear of Extinction: the fear of cessation, not existing anymore, dying, not alive.

Fear of Mutilation: the fear of loss of any body part

Fear of loss of Autonomy: the fear of being imprisoned in a place, not able to move around. To be curtailed, paralysed, or restricted, losing financial freedom etc.

Fear of Separation: the fear of being rejected, abandoned, left, not connected.

The fear of Ego-death: the fear of facing humiliation, loss of integrity, the feeling of shame and degradation. Losing a sense of worth.

Tips for dealing with fear

Understand your fears or what makes you feel scared and anxious. Every one of us has our own fears; some are afraid of heights, fear of riding a fast-moving vehicle, fear of being stuck in a limited space, fear of darkness, and fear of some animals. Your fear must not affect your everyday functioning. Understanding what makes you fearful can highlight you have a phobia. Some of the most common manifestation that you are fearful is a racing heartbeat, sweating, a feeling that you may faint or die, and dizziness. This fear might be rooted in some traumatic experiences from your past, mostly from childhood experiences. Understanding how fear manifests will give you an awareness that your fear is valid, and you must do something to address it.

Deal with your fear. Every time you feel that you are feeling anxious and are experiencing the symptoms mentioned earlier, it is imperative you know how to deal with it or to do something to ease the fear that you are feeling. Some of the suggested ways are to -

a) Breathe slowly and deeply. When you are fearful, your breathing isn't deep. You need to slow down your breathing and practice deep breathing. Make sure you are aware of your breathing.

b) Sometimes, we feel afraid because of negative thinking, so you must change your thoughts to deal with it. Be positive, think positive. Tell yourself,

"It's OK to relax" because you are the only one that can help yourself.

c) Leave the environment and get some fresh air; this may help reduce your anxiety. Taking a walk can help calm the nerves and help the individual relax.

Confront your fear; in Susan Jeffers book, Feel the fear and do it anyway. To deal with our fear, we must acknowledge the fear but still go ahead and do exactly what it is we are fearful of. If you are fearful of speaking in public, the best way to deal with that fear is to defy the fear and speak in public. As we confront our fear, it starts to diminish.

Reflection

Anger, when not managed, could prove self-destructive, and fear can become debilitating. These are two strong and negative emotions to watch out for.

Exercise

Continue with the last exercise from the previous day and note how frequent these two emotions of anger and fear come up.

Day 24

The Emotions of Happiness and Sadness

Happiness is a positive emotional state which can range from being content to being extremely joyful. You will agree with me that our main pursuit in life has an aim - to become happier. We get married, we have children, we have friends, we watch movies, and the list is endless. The more entertainment around, the more people are still looking for happiness, or so it seems.

Happiness has proved to be elusive; indeed, people in constant pursuit of happiness do not seem to have found it. Likewise, philosophers, psychologists are still trying to find the best way to define it. Why has happiness become so elusive? My thought is that we have built unrealistic expectations on what happiness should be. We think if we can have certain things we desire, we will be happy. This has led people to think it is money that can bring happiness. Understandably so, money can contribute to happiness, but it will not guarantee you are happy. I have seen a lot of poor, happy people and a lot of unhappy rich people. Some also think if they can achieve a particular goal, they will become happy, but as soon as the goal is accomplished, they set new ones, and the cycle continues. It has been proven scientifically that our choices determine over seventy per cent of our happiness. Don't think it is because you lack in some areas that is why you are unhappy; your happiness is a choice. Irrespective of your current situation or circumstance, you can still choose to be happy.

Truly I will repeat again for emphasis; Happiness is indeed a choice. I am particularly inspired by Nick Vujicic, a motivator, author, and evangelist who is living his best self despite not having arms and legs. Married with children, he did not allow what he did not have to get in the way of his happiness. A lot of people have arms and legs but are not able to accomplish a fifth of what he achieved. What is the difference? He made a choice to be happy, to be grateful for what he has and use it to his greatest advantage. He did not allow anything or anyone to get in his path of growth, happiness, and fulfilment.

The emotion sadness

Sadness, on the other hand, is the opposite of happiness. It is often characterised by feelings of loss, grief, or despair. When an individual is sad, he may choose to withdraw from others, he may become lethargic, and when it is severe, it can lead to depression. Depression is a serious illness and must be dealt with by professionals. When you feel sad occasionally, it is fine, but when it persists over a long period of time, quickly seek professional help to deal with whatever issue is making you sad. Depression not treated can lead to suicide. If you or anyone around you are beginning to self-harm or nursing thoughts of suicide, quickly seek professionals who are trained in the area to help you deal with it.

Tips for living a happier life

Don't compare yourself to others

It is better you don't compare yourself to others because comparing yourself to others can make you

135

miserable. In life, there will always be people you are better than and people better than you.

Be grateful

You don't have to have all your needs met before you can be thankful. Show appreciation for the life you have. Keep an appreciation diary. Write out a list of all you are thankful for daily. You will be amazed at all the things you can be thankful for.

Practice an act of kindness.

Doing things daily for people around you, showing an act of kindness within your community can make you happier. It has been scientifically proven that people who volunteer, working without getting paid, live longer and happier. It isn't saying that you spend your entire life working for nothing. Just find little things you can do that will make a big difference in people's life.

Getting regular exercises

Exercises are not only effective in improving our physical health but also our emotional health. When we exercise, the feel-good hormones are released, and this promotes a feeling of happiness and contentment.

When our physical health is improved, we are generally happier. Incorporating a simple routine as a daily walk can go a long way in helping with our emotions

Change your diet

If you are constantly unhappy for no apparent reason, you may also want to investigate your diet. As a rule, cut out sugar, eat more vegetables and fruits. Increase your essential fatty acids consumption by eating nuts and oily fish. You can supplement with cod liver oil or flaxseed oil. Consult your doctor before taking supplements, especially if you are on any medication.

Stay in a positive environment and around positive people

Staying around people who love and appreciate you is very important. Try as much as possible to stay away from negativity and negative people. Mind what you read, watch, or hear. Listen to inspiring words or messages.

Think positive

If you cannot think positive, you will always see the things that are not working. Therefore, changing how you view things will profoundly influence your emotional state, including how happy you are.

Reflection

You can make a choice today and decide to be happy irrespective of the current challenges.

Exercises

Make a list of all the things you are grateful for and say out aloud I am so thankful and happy for all these things.

Repeat the process for everything you are thankful for on your list.

Day 25

Be Mindful

"Mindfulness means being awake. It means knowing what you are doing." – Jon Kabat-Zinn

To become truly magnificent and live our ultimate life, it is important to know how to identify what are healthy and unhealthy thoughts and to weed out what is not helpful. One of the ways to do this is through mindfulness.

Mindfulness is a very powerful tool that can help us stay highly focused on the task at hand – It is an ability that we already possess. It's like our consciousness; we know where we are, what we are doing and what is happening. The key to mindfulness is understanding we are far more powerful than any negative thought, worry or imagined situation. A negative thought is useless in your external world unless you choose to make it into something more powerful than it is.

Benefits of Being Mindful

You will connect better with those around You-Being mindful will keep you in the here and now and help you improve communication and ultimately relationships with friends, family, and colleagues.

Your stress level will lower as it will help keep things in perspective. You will focus on now and not worry about what has passed or is to come.

Your mind will stay focused, and this keeps you on track.

Random thoughts in your mind will decrease, which drains our mental energy

You will embrace the future and forgive the past – knowing the past is gone and can't be changed, but there is something to look forward to in future.

Different Ways to Practise Mindfulness

Discover how to eat mindfully

Eating is one of life's little pleasures that we all do a few times a day, every day. Give your full attention to what you are eating. Don't watch the TV, look at the computer or study your phone. Embrace the tastes in your mouth. Focus on chewing your food thoroughly. Don't rush. Only think about the action and sensation of eating, nothing else. This puts the focus on your here and now. Not only will you improve your digestion, but this one little thing that you can practise quite a few times a day is teaching your brain to only concentrate on what you are doing and nothing more.

Take time to breathe

Our breathing is one of the greatest tools we have for practising mindfulness. It's consistent, regular, and always with us. Try to spend a few minutes a day concentrating on your breathing. Pay attention to it. You'll find that this technique will take you out of your thoughts and help you to realise that you are not your thoughts; you are the inner spirit.

Sweet showers and balmy bathing

At the end of a long day, or at the start of a new day, when you are bathing or showering, learn to enjoy the sensation of the water, the smells of your bathing gels or the feel of bubbles on your skin. Think only of what is with you at that one moment and really notice everything. Let your mind connect with the sensations and let all thoughts of everything else just slip away as you think only about what you are enjoying right now. If you do this at the start of the day, you will feel focused and ready for what the day will bring. If you do this at the end of the day, you are ready to unwind and prepare for a restful sleep.

Visualization

Visualization is like a dream, but you are controlling what you see while awake. To start visualizing, simply find a quiet and comfortable place, indoors or outdoors. Then, imagine yourself as being successful, you have achieved your goals, you can do anything you want to do. Focus only on that visualization. Let it embrace you. See how your life will be and feel those emotions. Don't think of anything else except your visual images. Visualization can also be used to help you overcome any obstacles you are facing. Visualize yourself overcoming the obstacle, dealing with it, and also learning from it. You may be surprised at what is inside your subconscious. The solutions are there, and by visualizing yourself overcoming any problems, you can offer yourself the tools to 'see' the solution.

Take mindful walks

Mindfulness can also be practised while you are walking somewhere. If you are walking to the shops, think only about what your eyes can see. Let your senses spring into life. What can you smell? What do these smells make you feel? Really look around you and focus on your surroundings and nothing else. If you are walking in a park or the countryside, enjoy the wildlife, the smell of the trees and flowers, the sound the grass makes when you walk. Don't get distracted by anything other than what is around you. Train your mind to embrace this one moment in time and concentrate on nothing else.

Reflection

Practising mindfulness is as necessary as working hard and staying positive for you to achieve what you want to achieve. It's not difficult to practise, as you have discovered, and the benefits are worth the effort of practising mindfulness.

"We have only now, only this single eternal moment opening and unfolding before us, day and night." – Jack Kornfield

Exercise

Sit in a quiet corner and start by focusing on your breathing. Once your thoughts start to wander, bring them back and concentrate again on your breathing. Do this for about five minutes.

Look around your house and focus on one thing at a time while also focusing on your breathing. Practice this for five to ten minutes.

Day 26

Synergise Your Effort

One thing you can do to achieve growth faster is connected and collaborate with others through Synergy. Synergy is derived from the Greek word, Synergos. This means "to work together" or "to collaborate. ". There is so much that can be achieved when you work with the right people who are connected to a common goal. According to the book of life -one will chase a thousand and two ten thousand.

One effective way of connecting and synergising your effort mentioned by Napoleon Hill in his book – Think and Grow Rich is Masterminding. Masterminding, to sum up, simply, is a gathering of people – usually two to six, but sometimes many more — who all connect around a common goal. This unity can result in a "chemistry" that is synergistic; individuals move forward as one person, and the total effect is greater than what would be possible for an individual acting alone. Masterminding can be a group of people focusing on one ultimate goal between them or a group who share ideas, concepts and help group members achieve their own goals. For example, you may need help raising finance, and one of the group members has this expertise or knows someone that can help you. The Mastermind is both the actual meeting of the minds, and the potential power available to everyone pulled together as one.

Groups – such as community groups, social media groups, business groups, and local groups- also leverage your efforts. If you have an idea, this can be improved through collective effort and collaboration. One very important step in developing innovative ideas is through creating a team made up of diverse people. The important thing about joining a group is to look for the one that is most relevant to your goal achievement. I have developed solid connections all over the world through this, which is the beauty of joining groups on social media- you are not limited to your local community. You will have support, opinions, and advice from others, make connections and be around like-minded people who also have the vision to make changes in their life or achieve goals that require dedication and hard work. You will all learn from each other. You will discover methods that can be successful, methods that don't work so well and methods that other group members are still trying out.

Things to do to get the best out of a group

Pick the appropriate one -It should serve the purpose of helping you achieve your goals.

Congruency matters- it is not only important for you to pick the one that helps in achieving your goal. You should also feel connected and comfortable in the group.

Be open- if you are struggling with any issue, don't be afraid or ashamed to ask questions; there will be one or two people who will be able to help. If you don't reach out, nobody will be able to help.

Reach out to others, contribute, and give- this will open doors of collaboration to you. Don't just be in a place to take; share your gift with others.

Get Coaching Support – Another way of synergising your effort is to hire a life coach. A good coach can help you achieve your goals faster than you would in years.

The investment is usually worth it. "Put your money where your mouth is" A coach will not only help you set goals, highlight your blind spots but will also make you accountable, form new habits and remove limiting beliefs. Like choosing a group to join, it is also important to choose a life coach you feel comfortable with for your investment to be worth it. Some coaches offer group coaching or one or one and some both.

Reflection

Working with like-minded people will help you in achieving your aims faster as you pull energy together towards the common aim.

Exercises

Look for groups you want to join, list them down and review each to determine suitability.

Set a date to join one and consider enrolling on a coaching program.

Day 27

Learn The Use of Affirmations

"It's the repetition of affirmations that leads to belief. And once that belief becomes a deep conviction, things begin to happen." - Claude M. Bristol

What you say about yourself is as important as what you think -Words are very powerful. It is not enough to think positive thoughts; these thoughts should be translated into words and the words into actions. Negative confessions can lead to depression, low self-esteem, unhappiness, and a retrogressive life. What you say and believe about yourself becomes a self-fulfilling prophecy as the subconscious mind does not understand the difference between fantasy and reality, negative or positive. We influence the universe with our spoken word. I believe every word we speak either direct energy towards us or against us. One way to challenge negative thought and self-sabotage is using "Affirmations".

Affirmations are powerful statements constructed to create positive mental images that aim to inspire, energize, and motivate. When we repeat affirmations to ourselves, they eventually go into our subconscious minds. The more we repeat these affirmations, the more it manifests. The aim is to train your mind into believing a positive affirmation and taking it as fact. That is why it is written in the holy book that faith comes by hearing and hearing by the word of God. The more you hear the word, the more you believe it and the more it works for you.

"I figured that if I said it enough, I would convince the world that I really was the greatest. "- Muhammad Ali

For affirmations to work, you must

1) Rid yourself of limiting beliefs and negative self-talk. You must believe that your positive declarations are not just ordinary words but have the power to transform your life. *"You will*

be a failure until you impress the subconscious with the conviction you are a success. This is done by making an AFFIRMATION which 'clicks' "- Florence Scovel Shinn

2) You must find an affirmation that triggers an emotional connection. It should address areas of your life where you want to experience changes. It may be to address certain challenges in some areas of your life or simply to find peace and tranquillity. For example, what goals are you aiming for? This should be clear enough. Is it success, good health, wealth, or emotional happiness?

3) You must train yourself to repeat your affirmations as often as possible. There is no point just glancing at them occasionally when you remember them. You train your subconscious to believe they are true, which will take a little time and practice. Try to set specific times of the day when you repeat your affirmations to yourself. Also, repeat them to yourself if you have doubtful or nagging voices in your head whispering negativity to you.

4) It is important that you believe in the power of affirmations. If you don't believe in them, they will lose their power to penetrate your subconscious, and the affirmations will not work.

5) Visualize your life as you see it when you have achieved your goals. Imagine how you might feel when you have achieved your goals or have achieved the first step of your final goal. How do you think you might feel? Visualize yourself with the ones you love, enjoying your life and feeling fulfilled. Eventually, the idea is to create your visualizations in your mind as soon as you repeat your affirmations to yourself or say them out loud. *"You must intensify and render continuous by repeatedly presenting with suggestive ideas and mental pictures of the feast of good things, and the flowing fountain, which awaits the successful achievement or attainment of the desires." - Robert Collier*

Common Affirmations you can adopt

Happiness

- I deserve to be happy
- Happiness is my birth right

- Happiness always finds me
- I am happy

Success

- I can achieve success easily and simply
- Success is flowing into my life every day
- Success is seeking me
- I am a magnet of success

Financial Wealth

- Everything I do attracts money
- Money is flowing into my life
- I am now earning a lot of money

Good Health

- My health is improving every day
- I am in good health and will remain in good health
- My body is full of the healing powers of the Universe

Self – Esteem

- I am magnificent
- I am a masterpiece of God's creation
- I am beautiful and wonderfully made

Reflection

Affirmations will help in reshaping our world as we continually impress our subconscious with powerful words. *"We cannot always control our thoughts, but we can control our words, and repetition impresses the subconscious, and we are then master of the situation."*— Jane Fonda

Exercises

List all the things you need to challenge in your life today.

Develop your own positive affirmations or adapt any suitable one. – Think about how to incorporate this into your daily routine.

Day 28

Deal with Self Sabotage

We have finally come to the last day of the journey to ultimate life. I believe we have learned a lot, and it is imperative to touch on a very important subject to maintaining our growth-and that is self-sabotage. Self-sabotage, in simple terms, is doing something that gets in the path of one's progress, deliberately "shooting off one's leg".

There are different reasons people self-sabotage, such as self-loathing, low self-esteem, superiority or inferiority complex, depression, anxiety etc. Also, it is possible to self-sabotage without realising it. The important thing is to identify why and when and work on it. To live the ultimate life and be truly magnificent, there are certain behaviours we must get rid of.

- Procrastination. Whatever needs to be done should be attended to instantly and should not be left till later. Procrastination can jeopardise jobs, relationships, and health. It is a destroyer of destiny.

- Another one to consider is lack of regard for time- you should never waste your time or other people's time as any time wasted can never be regained back.

- Maintain a good reputation, honour appointments- people should be able to trust you to deliver on your promises when you have an appointment to keep, arrive early. Promptness is the best possible proof that your own affairs are well ordered and well-conducted and gives others confidence in your ability. Anyone who is punctual, as a rule, will keep his word.

- Avoid addictive behaviours like excessive drinking self-medicating on drugs, inability to control the sexual urge.

- Avoid excessive talking, anger, acts of violence, quarrelsome attitude, indiscipline, and recklessness.

- Avoid lack of focus, unserious behaviour, tardiness.

- Avoid carefree attitude to health issues, lack of wisdom, keeping toxic relationships.
- Avoid false modesty, putting yourself down, being approval dependent, overly concerned about what others think of you and making decisions to please others.

Steps for dealing with self-sabotaging behaviours.

Step 1) **Awareness**

- Do a self-evaluation of yourself; acknowledge the fact that you self-sabotage.
- Write down all the ways you think you self-sabotage. Take your time and find a quiet place to do this uninterrupted. It is like clearing out the garbage inside and noting what your thoughts were when you engaged in self-sabotaging behaviours. This will shed more light on the underlying cause.

Step 2) **Own your thoughts and actions**

- You must now own your thoughts and take responsibility for your actions.

- Don't try to shift blame to others; accept you are the architect of your life. You are responsible for what you do and what you fail to do as well.

Step 3) **Commit to an action plan**

- Explore ways of stopping self-sabotaging behaviours.
- Write them down and select which you will likely commit to.
- To help you with this stage, you can get a friend or family to work with you or get a coach.
- Plan how you will respond to likely triggers
- Ensure you commit to your plan

Step 4) **Be Accountable**

- Share your plan with friends or family, so they can challenge you if you don't commit to your plan of action.
- People hire life coaches to get someone who is non-judgemental to assist in goal attainment through a concrete plan of action and accountability.

- Be open to feedback on your progress. Keep your motivation. Remind yourself of the benefits involved. Keep your eyes on the result; tell yourself you are worth the effort.

Step 5) **Motivate yourself**

- Don't get discouraged if the results are not fast enough.
- Engage in positive self-talk. Look into the mirror and tell yourself you can do it.
- Give yourself time to get results.
-

Step 6 **Celebrate milestones**

- Keep a diary to record progress
- Choose a day, week, or month to track progress.
- Create milestones for achievement and breakthrough.
- Positively reinforce the behaviour by choosing a reward.

Step 7) **Seek professional help**

Consider getting professional help if you think you are struggling and can't get the result you need. Different professionals can work with you, such as life coaches, social workers, therapists, and mental health professionals.

Reflection

Self-sabotage is like deliberately hurting yourself, and I am sure no one would want to do that. It is imperative to work on any self-sabotaging behaviours; we must maintain our magnificence and shine bright as the sun.

Exercise

Go over the steps for dealing with self-sabotage discussed above and make sure you devote time to the exercise working each step at a time.

Conclusion

The journey to living the Ultimate Life starts with you. The moment you realise you have the power to steer the course of your life, life takes on a new meaning. It is like being given a blank slate, and you are the writer -You are not just a powerless observer. Your mind is the seat of your power; it is the engine that drives your body. To change your life, you must change your thoughts.

You are created to be magnificent, but like the precious gem still buried within the ground, if you do not harness your gifts and utilise your strengths, you remain in obscurity and undiscovered. If again you hand over your personal power, you become like the chaff blown around by the wind, living at the whims and dictate of others.

You are the salt of this world, an important part of divine creation. Your assignment is important because it completes the overall picture of the world. You do not only owe it to yourself to live your full potentials, but it is also a duty to humanity. To solve the problem, you are created for and fulfil your life purpose.

You need to be also aware that the journey to ultimate life may not be easy. There will be roadblocks, discouragements; sometimes, you may even feel like quitting. Like gold, you may have to pass through the fire to refine your character and build resilience. It is all part of the story; your attitude will determine how you are able to pull through.

I want to encourage you with this word by **Friedrich *Nietzsche*** *"He who has a why to live for can bear almost any how."* If you know why you are doing what you are doing, you will be able to withstand the storm.

So, what are you going to do now? Continue to live your life the way you are, or you decide to upgrade to the next level and create the ultimate life where you shine in your magnificent brilliance. It is entirely your choice!

About the Author

Tolulope Olaniyan is a speaker, personal transformation coach and financial strategist. She has diverse qualifications in areas such as innovation, finance, insurance, business, training, and coaching but her passion is in supporting people to be the best they can be. She is passionate about change both within and outside and believes that leaders are not born but are made with the right tools and support.

As a speaker, Tolulope's areas of expertise include Personal transformation, Business development/ innovation, Personal Motivation, Emotional Intelligence, Financial Planning, Diversity, and Inclusion.

Tolulope lives in Navan, Co Meath in the Republic of Ireland with her three lovely children, who are not so young anymore. She is a mentor and coach to many young people and adults and has been involved in different life-changing community projects both within and outside Ireland.

Her organisation Pathways International Mission provides free coaching and empowerment support programs to children, women and young people in Africa aimed at alleviating poverty.

Tolulope loves to sing, read, and have a good phone chat in her spare time.

My personal motivation

Out of challenges and adversity, I discovered my purpose. My pain made me into who I am today, a better version of myself. I learned so many lessons, and perhaps the greatest is the battle within you. If you can overcome the battle from your mind, you have overcome the greatest battle. I realised that my greatest enemy was myself.

If you work on yourself first, every other area of your life starts to align. So, I dare you to take the challenge and create the world you dreamed of. If there is anything constant in life, it is change. So, lets' work together, change the world together through innovation, enterprise, and personal transformation.

Other Books and Services by the Author

The book is a guide for those who want to make positive changes in their life, transforming from the ordinary to the extraordinary. There is a latent power within everyone which you can call forth no matter your situation, even when you think you have completely messed up or have hit a dead end. You are faced with only two options: dare the challenge or fail. This book adopts a holistic approach to the mind, body, and spirit, guiding you through 21 winning steps that I used to transform my own life after my battle with emotional trauma. These steps are little changes you can make in your life that will produce phenomenal results. Life isn't a dress rehearsal; you only have one life to live. Live your life fully, live the life of your dreams, transform into your best self. FAME: Freedom Acceleration- Mastery- Empowerment.

Available on Amazon, Barnes and Nobles, Google books and others

The Ultimate Life Coaching Group – A free community of empowered people on Facebook

One More Thing Before You Go...

If you enjoyed reading this book or found it useful, I'd be very grateful if you'd post a short review on Amazon.

Your support really does make a difference, and I read all the reviews personally, so I can get your feedback and make this book even better.

If you would like to leave a review, then all you need to do is click the review link on Amazon here:https://amzn.to/3ClGdvv

And if you live in the UK, you can leave it here: https://amzn.to/30VEiWW

Thanks again for your support!

Printed in Great Britain
by Amazon